The New Business Road Test

The New Business Road Test

What entrepreneurs and executives should do
before writing a business plan

John W. Mullins

Prentice Hall
FINANCIAL TIMES

An imprint of Pearson Education

London ■ New York ■ San Francisco ■ Toronto ■ Sydney ■ Tokyo ■ Singapore
Hong Kong ■ Cape Town ■ Madrid ■ Amsterdam ■ Munich ■ Paris ■ Milan